THIS JOURNAL BOOK
BELONGS TO:

NAME: _____

ADDRESS: _____

_____

PHONE: _____

EMAIL: _____

COMPANY: _____

Hello There! Thank you for choosing this book. We hope you're enjoying it.

Please make sure to leave a review, we would definitely love to read your opinions and feedbacks, it will make us create better products for you in the futures.

To be kept up to date on future editions and other publications then please head over to www.vehok.com/kdp

Vehok Worldwide

TOWING INVOICE

COMPANY NAME	24 HOUR TOWING SERVICE FLATBED SERVICE
(STAMP)	REQ. BY:

NAME	DATE
ADDRESS	TIME

CITY	STATE	ZIP	PHONE

YEAR	MAKE / MODEL / COLOR	DRIVER

STATE	LIC NO.	VEHICLE ID NO.

☐ SLING/HOIST   ☐ FLAT TIRE

☐ WHEEL LIFT   ☐ OUT OF GAS

☐ FLAT BED/RAMP   ☐ WRECK

☐ START   ☐ RECOVERY

☐ LOCK OUT   ☐ ODOMETER READING

☐ BLOCK DRIVEWAY   ☐ ILLEGAL PARKING

SPECIAL EQUIPMENT

☐ SINGLE LINE WINCHING

☐ DUAL LINE WINCHING

☐ SNATCH BLOCKS

☐ SCOTCH BLOCKS

☐ DOLLY

☐ _____

LEFT SIDE   FRONT   BACK

RIGHT SIDE

I AUTHORIZE THE TOWING OF THE ABOVE VEHICLE

X _____

CAR WAS TOWED:

FROM:

TO:

MEMBER # _____

P.O.# _____

REMARKS _____

_____

_____

VEHICLE RELEASED TO _____

WITH NO FURTHER RECOURSE TO _____

DISTANCE TOWED:

MILEAGE END	
MILEAGE START	
TOTAL DISTANCE TOWED	
MILEAGE CHARGE	
TOWING CHARGE	
LABOR CHARGE	
STORAGE CHARGE	
TOLLS	
TAX	
TOTAL	

TOWING INVOICE

COMPANY NAME	**24 HOUR TOWING SERVICE** **FLATBED SERVICE**
(STAMP)	REQ. BY:
NAME	DATE
ADDRESS	TIME

CITY	STATE	ZIP	PHONE

YEAR	MAKE / MODEL / COLOR	DRIVER

STATE	LIC NO.	VEHICLE ID NO.	

☐ SLING/HOIST   ☐ FLAT TIRE

☐ WHEEL LIFT   ☐ OUT OF GAS

☐ FLAT BED/RAMP   ☐ WRECK

☐ START   ☐ RECOVERY

☐ LOCK OUT   ☐ ODOMETER READING

☐ BLOCK DRIVEWAY   ☐ ILLEGAL PARKING

SPECIAL EQUIPMENT

☐ SINGLE LINE WINCHING

☐ DUAL LINE WINCHING

☐ SNATCH BLOCKS

☐ SCOTCH BLOCKS

☐ DOLLY

☐ _____

LEFT SIDE

FRONT

BACK

RIGHT SIDE

I AUTHORIZE THE TOWING OF THE ABOVE VEHICLE

X _____

CAR WAS TOWED: **DISTANCE TOWED:**

FROM:	MILEAGE END	
TO:	MILEAGE START	
	TOTAL DISTANCE TOWED	
MEMBER # _____	MILEAGE CHARGE	
P.O.# _____	TOWING CHARGE	
REMARKS _____	LABOR CHARGE	
_____	STORAGE CHARGE	
_____	TOLLS	
VEHICLE RELEASED TO _____	TAX	
WITH NO FURTHER RECOURSE TO _____	**TOTAL**	

TOWING INVOICE

COMPANY NAME	24 HOUR TOWING SERVICE FLATBED SERVICE	
	REQ. BY:	
(STAMP)		

NAME	DATE
ADDRESS	TIME

CITY	STATE	ZIP	PHONE

YEAR	MAKE / MODEL / COLOR	DRIVER

STATE	LIC NO.	VEHICLE ID NO.	

☐ SLING/HOIST   ☐ FLAT TIRE

☐ WHEEL LIFT   ☐ OUT OF GAS

☐ FLAT BED/RAMP   ☐ WRECK

☐ START   ☐ RECOVERY

☐ LOCK OUT   ☐ ODOMETER READING

☐ BLOCK DRIVEWAY   ☐ ILLEGAL PARKING

SPECIAL EQUIPMENT

☐ SINGLE LINE WINCHING

☐ DUAL LINE WINCHING

☐ SNATCH BLOCKS

☐ SCOTCH BLOCKS

☐ DOLLY

☐ _____

LEFT SIDE   FRONT   BACK

RIGHT SIDE

I AUTHORIZE THE TOWING OF THE ABOVE VEHICLE

X _____

CAR WAS TOWED:

DISTANCE TOWED:

FROM:	MILEAGE END	
TO:	MILEAGE START	
	TOTAL DISTANCE TOWED	
MEMBER # _____	MILEAGE CHARGE	
P.O.# _____	TOWING CHARGE	
REMARKS _____	LABOR CHARGE	
_____	STORAGE CHARGE	
_____	TOLLS	
VEHICLE RELEASED TO _____	TAX	
WITH NO FURTHER RECOURSE TO ____		
	TOTAL	

TOWING INVOICE

COMPANY NAME	24 HOUR TOWING SERVICE FLATBED SERVICE

	REQ. BY:
NAME	DATE
ADDRESS	TIME

CITY	STATE	ZIP	PHONE

YEAR	MAKE / MODEL / COLOR	DRIVER

STATE	LIC NO.	VEHICLE ID NO.

- ☐ SLING/HOIST
- ☐ WHEEL LIFT
- ☐ FLAT BED/RAMP
- ☐ START
- ☐ LOCK OUT
- ☐ BLOCK DRIVEWAY

- ☐ FLAT TIRE
- ☐ OUT OF GAS
- ☐ WRECK
- ☐ RECOVERY
- ☐ ODOMETER READING
- ☐ ILLEGAL PARKING

SPECIAL EQUIPMENT
- ☐ SINGLE LINE WINCHING
- ☐ DUAL LINE WINCHING
- ☐ SNATCH BLOCKS
- ☐ SCOTCH BLOCKS
- ☐ DOLLY
- ☐ _____

LEFT SIDE

FRONT

BACK

RIGHT SIDE

I AUTHORIZE THE TOWING OF THE ABOVE VEHICLE

X _____

CAR WAS TOWED:	DISTANCE TOWED:	
FROM:	MILEAGE END	
TO:	MILEAGE START	
	TOTAL DISTANCE TOWED	
MEMBER # _____	MILEAGE CHARGE	
P.O.# _____	TOWING CHARGE	
REMARKS _____	LABOR CHARGE	
_____	STORAGE CHARGE	
_____	TOLLS	
VEHICLE RELEASED TO _____	TAX	
WITH NO FURTHER RECOURSE TO _____		
	TOTAL	

TOWING INVOICE

COMPANY NAME		24 HOUR TOWING SERVICE FLATBED SERVICE
	(STAMP)	REQ. BY:
NAME		DATE
ADDRESS		TIME
CITY	STATE	ZIP	PHONE
YEAR	MAKE / MODEL / COLOR	DRIVER
STATE	LIC NO.	VEHICLE ID NO.	

- ☐ SLING/HOIST
- ☐ WHEEL LIFT
- ☐ FLAT BED/RAMP
- ☐ START
- ☐ LOCK OUT
- ☐ BLOCK DRIVEWAY

- ☐ FLAT TIRE
- ☐ OUT OF GAS
- ☐ WRECK
- ☐ RECOVERY
- ☐ ODOMETER READING
- ☐ ILLEGAL PARKING

SPECIAL EQUIPMENT
- ☐ SINGLE LINE WINCHING
- ☐ DUAL LINE WINCHING
- ☐ SNATCH BLOCKS
- ☐ SCOTCH BLOCKS
- ☐ DOLLY
- ☐ _____

LEFT SIDE

FRONT

BACK

RIGHT SIDE

I AUTHORIZE THE TOWING OF THE ABOVE VEHICLE

X _____

CAR WAS TOWED:	DISTANCE TOWED:	
FROM:	MILEAGE END	
TO:	MILEAGE START	
	TOTAL DISTANCE TOWED	
MEMBER # _____	MILEAGE CHARGE	
P.O.# _____	TOWING CHARGE	
REMARKS _____	LABOR CHARGE	
_____	STORAGE CHARGE	
VEHICLE RELEASED TO _____	TOLLS	
WITH NO FURTHER RECOURSE TO ___	TAX	
	TOTAL	

TOWING INVOICE

COMPANY NAME		**24 HOUR TOWING SERVICE FLATBED SERVICE**
	(STAMP)	REQ. BY:
NAME		DATE
ADDRESS		TIME
CITY	STATE	ZIP	PHONE
YEAR	MAKE / MODEL / COLOR		DRIVER
STATE	LIC NO.	VEHICLE ID NO.	

☐ SLING/HOIST ☐ FLAT TIRE
☐ WHEEL LIFT ☐ OUT OF GAS
☐ FLAT BED/RAMP ☐ WRECK
☐ START ☐ RECOVERY
☐ LOCK OUT ☐ ODOMETER READING
☐ BLOCK DRIVEWAY ☐ ILLEGAL PARKING

SPECIAL EQUIPMENT
☐ SINGLE LINE WINCHING
☐ DUAL LINE WINCHING
☐ SNATCH BLOCKS
☐ SCOTCH BLOCKS
☐ DOLLY
☐ _____

LEFT SIDE

FRONT

BACK

RIGHT SIDE

I AUTHORIZE THE TOWING OF THE ABOVE VEHICLE

X _____

CAR WAS TOWED:

FROM:

TO:

MEMBER # _____

P.O.# _____

REMARKS _____
_____
_____

VEHICLE RELEASED TO _____
WITH NO FURTHER RECOURSE TO _____

DISTANCE TOWED:

MILEAGE END	
MILEAGE START	
TOTAL DISTANCE TOWED	
MILEAGE CHARGE	
TOWING CHARGE	
LABOR CHARGE	
STORAGE CHARGE	
TOLLS	
TAX	
TOTAL	

TOWING INVOICE

COMPANY NAME	**24 HOUR TOWING SERVICE FLATBED SERVICE**
(STAMP)	REQ. BY:
NAME	DATE
ADDRESS	TIME

CITY	STATE	ZIP	PHONE

YEAR	MAKE / MODEL / COLOR	DRIVER

STATE	LIC NO.	VEHICLE ID NO.

- ☐ SLING/HOIST
- ☐ WHEEL LIFT
- ☐ FLAT BED/RAMP
- ☐ START
- ☐ LOCK OUT
- ☐ BLOCK DRIVEWAY

- ☐ FLAT TIRE
- ☐ OUT OF GAS
- ☐ WRECK
- ☐ RECOVERY
- ☐ ODOMETER READING
- ☐ ILLEGAL PARKING

SPECIAL EQUIPMENT
- ☐ SINGLE LINE WINCHING
- ☐ DUAL LINE WINCHING
- ☐ SNATCH BLOCKS
- ☐ SCOTCH BLOCKS
- ☐ DOLLY
- ☐ _____

LEFT SIDE

FRONT

BACK

RIGHT SIDE

I AUTHORIZE THE TOWING OF THE ABOVE VEHICLE

X _____

CAR WAS TOWED:

FROM:

TO:

MEMBER # _____

P.O.# _____

REMARKS _____

_____

_____

VEHICLE RELEASED TO _____
WITH NO FURTHER RECOURSE TO _____

DISTANCE TOWED:	
MILEAGE END	
MILEAGE START	
TOTAL DISTANCE TOWED	
MILEAGE CHARGE	
TOWING CHARGE	
LABOR CHARGE	
STORAGE CHARGE	
TOLLS	
TAX	
TOTAL	

TOWING INVOICE

COMPANY NAME			**24 HOUR TOWING SERVICE** **FLATBED SERVICE**	
			REQ. BY:	
	(STAMP)			
NAME			DATE	
ADDRESS			TIME	
CITY	STATE	ZIP	PHONE	
YEAR	MAKE / MODEL / COLOR		DRIVER	
STATE	LIC NO.	VEHICLE ID NO.		

- ☐ SLING/HOIST
- ☐ WHEEL LIFT
- ☐ FLAT BED/RAMP
- ☐ START
- ☐ LOCK OUT
- ☐ BLOCK DRIVEWAY

- ☐ FLAT TIRE
- ☐ OUT OF GAS
- ☐ WRECK
- ☐ RECOVERY
- ☐ ODOMETER READING
- ☐ ILLEGAL PARKING

SPECIAL EQUIPMENT
- ☐ SINGLE LINE WINCHING
- ☐ DUAL LINE WINCHING
- ☐ SNATCH BLOCKS
- ☐ SCOTCH BLOCKS
- ☐ DOLLY
- ☐ _____

LEFT SIDE

FRONT

BACK

RIGHT SIDE

I AUTHORIZE THE TOWING OF
THE ABOVE VEHICLE

X _____

CAR WAS TOWED:	DISTANCE TOWED:	
FROM:	MILEAGE END	
TO:	MILEAGE START	
	TOTAL DISTANCE TOWED	
MEMBER # _____	MILEAGE CHARGE	
P.O.# _____	TOWING CHARGE	
REMARKS _____	LABOR CHARGE	
_____	STORAGE CHARGE	
_____	TOLLS	
VEHICLE RELEASED TO _____	TAX	
WITH NO FURTHER RECOURSE TO _____	**TOTAL**	

TOWING INVOICE

COMPANY NAME	**24 HOUR TOWING SERVICE** **FLATBED SERVICE**
(STAMP)	REQ. BY:
NAME	DATE
ADDRESS	TIME

CITY	STATE	ZIP	PHONE
YEAR	MAKE / MODEL / COLOR		DRIVER
STATE	LIC NO.	VEHICLE ID NO.	

☐ SLING/HOIST   ☐ FLAT TIRE   **SPECIAL EQUIPMENT**
☐ WHEEL LIFT   ☐ OUT OF GAS   ☐ SINGLE LINE WINCHING
☐ FLAT BED/RAMP   ☐ WRECK   ☐ DUAL LINE WINCHING
☐ START   ☐ RECOVERY   ☐ SNATCH BLOCKS
☐ LOCK OUT   ☐ ODOMETER READING   ☐ SCOTCH BLOCKS
☐ BLOCK DRIVEWAY   ☐ ILLEGAL PARKING   ☐ DOLLY
    ☐ _____

LEFT SIDE   FRONT   BACK

RIGHT SIDE

I AUTHORIZE THE TOWING OF THE ABOVE VEHICLE

X _____

CAR WAS TOWED:	**DISTANCE TOWED:**	
FROM:	MILEAGE END	
TO:	MILEAGE START	
	TOTAL DISTANCE TOWED	
MEMBER # _____	MILEAGE CHARGE	
P.O.# _____	TOWING CHARGE	
REMARKS _____	LABOR CHARGE	
_____	STORAGE CHARGE	
_____	TOLLS	
VEHICLE RELEASED TO _____	TOLLS	
WITH NO FURTHER RECOURSE TO _____	TAX	
	TOTAL	

TOWING INVOICE

COMPANY NAME		**24 HOUR TOWING SERVICE**
		FLATBED SERVICE
(STAMP)		REQ. BY:
NAME		DATE
ADDRESS		TIME
CITY	STATE	ZIP	PHONE
YEAR	MAKE / MODEL / COLOR	DRIVER
STATE	LIC NO.	VEHICLE ID NO.	

- ☐ SLING/HOIST
- ☐ WHEEL LIFT
- ☐ FLAT BED/RAMP
- ☐ START
- ☐ LOCK OUT
- ☐ BLOCK DRIVEWAY

- ☐ FLAT TIRE
- ☐ OUT OF GAS
- ☐ WRECK
- ☐ RECOVERY
- ☐ ODOMETER READING
- ☐ ILLEGAL PARKING

SPECIAL EQUIPMENT
- ☐ SINGLE LINE WINCHING
- ☐ DUAL LINE WINCHING
- ☐ SNATCH BLOCKS
- ☐ SCOTCH BLOCKS
- ☐ DOLLY
- ☐ _____

LEFT SIDE

FRONT

BACK

RIGHT SIDE

I AUTHORIZE THE TOWING OF
THE ABOVE VEHICLE

X _____

CAR WAS TOWED: | DISTANCE TOWED:

FROM:	MILEAGE END
TO:	MILEAGE START
	TOTAL DISTANCE TOWED
MEMBER # _____	MILEAGE CHARGE
P.O.# _____	TOWING CHARGE
REMARKS _____	LABOR CHARGE
_____	STORAGE CHARGE
_____	TOLLS
VEHICLE RELEASED TO _____	TAX
WITH NO FURTHER RECOURSE TO _____	
	TOTAL

TOWING INVOICE

COMPANY NAME					**24 HOUR TOWING SERVICE**
					FLATBED SERVICE
				(STAMP)	REQ. BY:
NAME					DATE
ADDRESS					TIME
CITY		STATE		ZIP	PHONE
YEAR	MAKE / MODEL / COLOR				DRIVER
STATE	LIC NO.		VEHICLE ID NO.		

- ☐ SLING/HOIST
- ☐ WHEEL LIFT
- ☐ FLAT BED/RAMP
- ☐ START
- ☐ LOCK OUT
- ☐ BLOCK DRIVEWAY

- ☐ FLAT TIRE
- ☐ OUT OF GAS
- ☐ WRECK
- ☐ RECOVERY
- ☐ ODOMETER READING
- ☐ ILLEGAL PARKING

SPECIAL EQUIPMENT
- ☐ SINGLE LINE WINCHING
- ☐ DUAL LINE WINCHING
- ☐ SNATCH BLOCKS
- ☐ SCOTCH BLOCKS
- ☐ DOLLY
- ☐ _____

LEFT SIDE

FRONT

BACK

RIGHT SIDE

I AUTHORIZE THE TOWING OF THE ABOVE VEHICLE

X _____

CAR WAS TOWED:	DISTANCE TOWED:	
FROM:	MILEAGE END	
TO:	MILEAGE START	
	TOTAL DISTANCE TOWED	
MEMBER # _____	MILEAGE CHARGE	
P.O.# _____	TOWING CHARGE	
REMARKS _____	LABOR CHARGE	
_____	STORAGE CHARGE	
_____	TOLLS	
VEHICLE RELEASED TO _____	TOLLS	
WITH NO FURTHER RECOURSE TO _____	TAX	
	TOTAL	

TOWING INVOICE

COMPANY NAME	**24 HOUR TOWING SERVICE** **FLATBED SERVICE**
	REQ. BY:
(STAMP)	
NAME	DATE
ADDRESS	TIME

CITY	STATE	ZIP	PHONE

YEAR	MAKE / MODEL / COLOR	DRIVER
STATE	LIC NO.	VEHICLE ID NO.

- ☐ SLING/HOIST
- ☐ WHEEL LIFT
- ☐ FLAT BED/RAMP
- ☐ START
- ☐ LOCK OUT
- ☐ BLOCK DRIVEWAY

- ☐ FLAT TIRE
- ☐ OUT OF GAS
- ☐ WRECK
- ☐ RECOVERY
- ☐ ODOMETER READING
- ☐ ILLEGAL PARKING

SPECIAL EQUIPMENT
- ☐ SINGLE LINE WINCHING
- ☐ DUAL LINE WINCHING
- ☐ SNATCH BLOCKS
- ☐ SCOTCH BLOCKS
- ☐ DOLLY
- ☐ _____

LEFT SIDE

FRONT

BACK

RIGHT SIDE

I AUTHORIZE THE TOWING OF THE ABOVE VEHICLE

X _____

CAR WAS TOWED:

FROM:

TO:

MEMBER # _____

P.O.# _____

REMARKS _____

_____

_____

VEHICLE RELEASED TO _____
WITH NO FURTHER RECOURSE TO _____

DISTANCE TOWED:

MILEAGE END	
MILEAGE START	
TOTAL DISTANCE TOWED	
MILEAGE CHARGE	
TOWING CHARGE	
LABOR CHARGE	
STORAGE CHARGE	
TOLLS	
TAX	
TOTAL	

TOWING INVOICE

COMPANY NAME	**24 HOUR TOWING SERVICE FLATBED SERVICE**
(STAMP)	REQ. BY:
NAME	DATE
ADDRESS	TIME

CITY	STATE	ZIP	PHONE

YEAR	MAKE / MODEL / COLOR	DRIVER

STATE	LIC NO.	VEHICLE ID NO.

☐ SLING/HOIST   ☐ FLAT TIRE

☐ WHEEL LIFT   ☐ OUT OF GAS

☐ FLAT BED/RAMP   ☐ WRECK

☐ START   ☐ RECOVERY

☐ LOCK OUT   ☐ ODOMETER READING

☐ BLOCK DRIVEWAY   ☐ ILLEGAL PARKING

SPECIAL EQUIPMENT

☐ SINGLE LINE WINCHING

☐ DUAL LINE WINCHING

☐ SNATCH BLOCKS

☐ SCOTCH BLOCKS

☐ DOLLY

☐ _____

LEFT SIDE   FRONT   BACK

RIGHT SIDE

I AUTHORIZE THE TOWING OF THE ABOVE VEHICLE

X _____

CAR WAS TOWED:	**DISTANCE TOWED:**	
FROM:	MILEAGE END	
TO:	MILEAGE START	
	TOTAL DISTANCE TOWED	
MEMBER # _____	MILEAGE CHARGE	
P.O.# _____	TOWING CHARGE	
REMARKS _____	LABOR CHARGE	
_____	STORAGE CHARGE	
_____	TOLLS	
VEHICLE RELEASED TO _____	TAX	
WITH NO FURTHER RECOURSE TO _____	**TOTAL**	

TOWING INVOICE

COMPANY NAME		**24 HOUR TOWING SERVICE** **FLATBED SERVICE**
	(STAMP)	REQ. BY:
NAME		DATE
ADDRESS		TIME
CITY	STATE	ZIP	PHONE
YEAR	MAKE / MODEL / COLOR	DRIVER
STATE	LIC NO.	VEHICLE ID NO.

☐ SLING/HOIST ☐ FLAT TIRE **SPECIAL EQUIPMENT**
☐ WHEEL LIFT ☐ OUT OF GAS ☐ SINGLE LINE WINCHING
☐ FLAT BED/RAMP ☐ WRECK ☐ DUAL LINE WINCHING
☐ START ☐ RECOVERY ☐ SNATCH BLOCKS
☐ LOCK OUT ☐ ODOMETER READING ☐ SCOTCH BLOCKS
☐ BLOCK DRIVEWAY ☐ ILLEGAL PARKING ☐ DOLLY
☐ _____

LEFT SIDE   FRONT   BACK

RIGHT SIDE

I AUTHORIZE THE TOWING OF THE ABOVE VEHICLE

X _____

CAR WAS TOWED:	DISTANCE TOWED:	
FROM:	MILEAGE END	
TO:	MILEAGE START	
	TOTAL DISTANCE TOWED	
MEMBER # _____	MILEAGE CHARGE	
P.O.# _____	TOWING CHARGE	
REMARKS _____	LABOR CHARGE	
_____	STORAGE CHARGE	
_____	TOLLS	
VEHICLE RELEASED TO _____	TAX	
WITH NO FURTHER RECOURSE TO _____	TOTAL	

TOWING INVOICE

COMPANY NAME (STAMP)	**24 HOUR TOWING SERVICE** **FLATBED SERVICE**

NAME				**REQ. BY:**
ADDRESS				**DATE**
CITY	**STATE**	**ZIP**		**TIME**
YEAR	**MAKE / MODEL / COLOR**			**PHONE**
STATE	**LIC NO.**	**VEHICLE ID NO.**		**DRIVER**

☐ SLING/HOIST   ☐ FLAT TIRE   **SPECIAL EQUIPMENT**
☐ WHEEL LIFT   ☐ OUT OF GAS   ☐ SINGLE LINE WINCHING
☐ FLAT BED/RAMP   ☐ WRECK   ☐ DUAL LINE WINCHING
☐ START   ☐ RECOVERY   ☐ SNATCH BLOCKS
☐ LOCK OUT   ☐ ODOMETER READING ☐ SCOTCH BLOCKS
☐ BLOCK DRIVEWAY   ☐ ILLEGAL PARKING   ☐ DOLLY
                                     ☐ _____

LEFT SIDE   FRONT   BACK

RIGHT SIDE

I AUTHORIZE THE TOWING OF THE ABOVE VEHICLE

X _____

CAR WAS TOWED:	**DISTANCE TOWED:**	
FROM:	**MILEAGE END**	
TO:	**MILEAGE START**	
	TOTAL DISTANCE TOWED	
MEMBER # _____	**MILEAGE CHARGE**	
P.O.# _____	**TOWING CHARGE**	
REMARKS _____	**LABOR CHARGE**	
_____	**STORAGE CHARGE**	
_____	**TOLLS**	
VEHICLE RELEASED TO _____	**TAX**	
WITH NO FURTHER RECOURSE TO _____	**TOTAL**	

TOWING INVOICE

COMPANY NAME	24 HOUR TOWING SERVICE FLATBED SERVICE
(STAMP)	REQ. BY:
NAME	DATE
ADDRESS	TIME

CITY	STATE	ZIP	PHONE

YEAR	MAKE / MODEL / COLOR	DRIVER

STATE	LIC NO.	VEHICLE ID NO.

- ☐ SLING/HOIST
- ☐ WHEEL LIFT
- ☐ FLAT BED/RAMP
- ☐ START
- ☐ LOCK OUT
- ☐ BLOCK DRIVEWAY

- ☐ FLAT TIRE
- ☐ OUT OF GAS
- ☐ WRECK
- ☐ RECOVERY
- ☐ ODOMETER READING
- ☐ ILLEGAL PARKING

SPECIAL EQUIPMENT
- ☐ SINGLE LINE WINCHING
- ☐ DUAL LINE WINCHING
- ☐ SNATCH BLOCKS
- ☐ SCOTCH BLOCKS
- ☐ DOLLY
- ☐ _____

LEFT SIDE

FRONT

BACK

RIGHT SIDE

I AUTHORIZE THE TOWING OF THE ABOVE VEHICLE

X _____

CAR WAS TOWED:	DISTANCE TOWED:	
FROM:	MILEAGE END	
TO:	MILEAGE START	
	TOTAL DISTANCE TOWED	
MEMBER # _____	MILEAGE CHARGE	
P.O.# _____	TOWING CHARGE	
REMARKS _____	LABOR CHARGE	
_____	STORAGE CHARGE	
_____	TOLLS	
VEHICLE RELEASED TO _____	TAX	
WITH NO FURTHER RECOURSE TO _____	TOTAL	

TOWING INVOICE

COMPANY NAME	24 HOUR TOWING SERVICE FLATBED SERVICE	
	REQ. BY:	
(STAMP)		

NAME	DATE
ADDRESS	TIME

CITY	STATE	ZIP	PHONE

YEAR	MAKE / MODEL / COLOR	DRIVER

STATE	LIC NO.	VEHICLE ID NO.

☐ SLING/HOIST   ☐ FLAT TIRE

☐ WHEEL LIFT   ☐ OUT OF GAS

☐ FLAT BED/RAMP   ☐ WRECK

☐ START   ☐ RECOVERY

☐ LOCK OUT   ☐ ODOMETER READING

☐ BLOCK DRIVEWAY   ☐ ILLEGAL PARKING

SPECIAL EQUIPMENT

☐ SINGLE LINE WINCHING

☐ DUAL LINE WINCHING

☐ SNATCH BLOCKS

☐ SCOTCH BLOCKS

☐ DOLLY

☐ _____

LEFT SIDE   FRONT   BACK

RIGHT SIDE

I AUTHORIZE THE TOWING OF THE ABOVE VEHICLE

X _____

CAR WAS TOWED:	DISTANCE TOWED:	
FROM:	MILEAGE END	
TO:	MILEAGE START	
	TOTAL DISTANCE TOWED	
MEMBER # _____	MILEAGE CHARGE	
P.O.# _____	TOWING CHARGE	
REMARKS _____	LABOR CHARGE	
_____	STORAGE CHARGE	
_____	TOLLS	
VEHICLE RELEASED TO _____	TAX	
WITH NO FURTHER RECOURSE TO _____	**TOTAL**	

TOWING INVOICE

COMPANY NAME	24 HOUR TOWING SERVICE FLATBED SERVICE
(STAMP)	REQ. BY:
NAME	DATE
ADDRESS	TIME

CITY	STATE	ZIP	PHONE

YEAR	MAKE / MODEL / COLOR	DRIVER

STATE	LIC NO.	VEHICLE ID NO.

☐ SLING/HOIST   ☐ FLAT TIRE

☐ WHEEL LIFT   ☐ OUT OF GAS

☐ FLAT BED/RAMP   ☐ WRECK

☐ START   ☐ RECOVERY

☐ LOCK OUT   ☐ ODOMETER READING

☐ BLOCK DRIVEWAY   ☐ ILLEGAL PARKING

SPECIAL EQUIPMENT

☐ SINGLE LINE WINCHING

☐ DUAL LINE WINCHING

☐ SNATCH BLOCKS

☐ SCOTCH BLOCKS

☐ DOLLY

☐ _____

LEFT SIDE   FRONT   BACK

RIGHT SIDE

I AUTHORIZE THE TOWING OF THE ABOVE VEHICLE

X _____

CAR WAS TOWED:

FROM: _____

TO: _____

MEMBER # _____

P.O.# _____

REMARKS _____

_____

_____

VEHICLE RELEASED TO _____

WITH NO FURTHER RECOURSE TO _____

DISTANCE TOWED:	
MILEAGE END	
MILEAGE START	
TOTAL DISTANCE TOWED	
MILEAGE CHARGE	
TOWING CHARGE	
LABOR CHARGE	
STORAGE CHARGE	
TOLLS	
TAX	
TOTAL	

TOWING INVOICE

COMPANY NAME		24 HOUR TOWING SERVICE FLATBED SERVICE	
	(STAMP)	REQ. BY:	
NAME		DATE	
ADDRESS		TIME	
CITY	STATE / ZIP	PHONE	
YEAR	MAKE / MODEL / COLOR	DRIVER	
STATE	LIC NO. / VEHICLE ID NO.		

☐ SLING/HOIST   ☐ FLAT TIRE   **SPECIAL EQUIPMENT**
☐ WHEEL LIFT   ☐ OUT OF GAS   ☐ SINGLE LINE WINCHING
☐ FLAT BED/RAMP   ☐ WRECK   ☐ DUAL LINE WINCHING
☐ START   ☐ RECOVERY   ☐ SNATCH BLOCKS
☐ LOCK OUT   ☐ ODOMETER READING   ☐ SCOTCH BLOCKS
☐ BLOCK DRIVEWAY   ☐ ILLEGAL PARKING   ☐ DOLLY
    ☐ _____

LEFT SIDE   FRONT   BACK

RIGHT SIDE

I AUTHORIZE THE TOWING OF THE ABOVE VEHICLE

X _____

CAR WAS TOWED:	DISTANCE TOWED:	
FROM:	MILEAGE END	
TO:	MILEAGE START	
	TOTAL DISTANCE TOWED	
MEMBER # _____	MILEAGE CHARGE	
P.O.# _____	TOWING CHARGE	
REMARKS _____	LABOR CHARGE	
_____	STORAGE CHARGE	
_____	TOLLS	
VEHICLE RELEASED TO _____	TAX	
WITH NO FURTHER RECOURSE TO _____	**TOTAL**	

TOWING INVOICE

COMPANY NAME		24 HOUR TOWING SERVICE FLATBED SERVICE
	(STAMP)	REQ. BY:
NAME		DATE
ADDRESS		TIME
CITY	STATE	ZIP	PHONE
YEAR	MAKE / MODEL / COLOR	DRIVER
STATE	LIC NO.	VEHICLE ID NO.

☐ SLING/HOIST   ☐ FLAT TIRE

☐ WHEEL LIFT   ☐ OUT OF GAS

☐ FLAT BED/RAMP   ☐ WRECK

☐ START   ☐ RECOVERY

☐ LOCK OUT   ☐ ODOMETER READING

☐ BLOCK DRIVEWAY   ☐ ILLEGAL PARKING

SPECIAL EQUIPMENT

☐ SINGLE LINE WINCHING

☐ DUAL LINE WINCHING

☐ SNATCH BLOCKS

☐ SCOTCH BLOCKS

☐ DOLLY

☐ _____

LEFT SIDE   FRONT   BACK

RIGHT SIDE

I AUTHORIZE THE TOWING OF THE ABOVE VEHICLE

X _____

CAR WAS TOWED:	DISTANCE TOWED:	
FROM:	MILEAGE END	
TO:	MILEAGE START	
	TOTAL DISTANCE TOWED	
MEMBER # _____	MILEAGE CHARGE	
P.O.# _____	TOWING CHARGE	
REMARKS _____	LABOR CHARGE	
_____	STORAGE CHARGE	
_____	TOLLS	
VEHICLE RELEASED TO _____	TAX	
WITH NO FURTHER RECOURSE TO _____	TOTAL	

TOWING INVOICE

COMPANY NAME		24 HOUR TOWING SERVICE FLATBED SERVICE	
	(STAMP)	REQ. BY:	
NAME		DATE	
ADDRESS		TIME	
CITY	STATE / ZIP	PHONE	
YEAR / MAKE / MODEL / COLOR		DRIVER	
STATE / LIC NO. / VEHICLE ID NO.			

☐ SLING/HOIST   ☐ FLAT TIRE
☐ WHEEL LIFT   ☐ OUT OF GAS
☐ FLAT BED/RAMP   ☐ WRECK
☐ START   ☐ RECOVERY
☐ LOCK OUT   ☐ ODOMETER READING
☐ BLOCK DRIVEWAY ☐ ILLEGAL PARKING

SPECIAL EQUIPMENT
☐ SINGLE LINE WINCHING
☐ DUAL LINE WINCHING
☐ SNATCH BLOCKS
☐ SCOTCH BLOCKS
☐ DOLLY
☐ _____

LEFT SIDE   FRONT   BACK

RIGHT SIDE

I AUTHORIZE THE TOWING OF THE ABOVE VEHICLE

X _____

CAR WAS TOWED:	DISTANCE TOWED:	
FROM:	MILEAGE END	
TO:	MILEAGE START	
	TOTAL DISTANCE TOWED	
MEMBER # _____	MILEAGE CHARGE	
P.O.# _____	TOWING CHARGE	
REMARKS _____	LABOR CHARGE	
_____	STORAGE CHARGE	
_____	TOLLS	
VEHICLE RELEASED TO _____	TAX	
WITH NO FURTHER RECOURSE TO _____	TOTAL	

TOWING INVOICE

COMPANY NAME	24 HOUR TOWING SERVICE FLATBED SERVICE
(STAMP)	REQ. BY:

NAME	DATE
ADDRESS	TIME

CITY	STATE	ZIP	PHONE

YEAR	MAKE / MODEL / COLOR	DRIVER

STATE	LIC NO.	VEHICLE ID NO.	

☐ SLING/HOIST   ☐ FLAT TIRE

☐ WHEEL LIFT   ☐ OUT OF GAS

☐ FLAT BED/RAMP   ☐ WRECK

☐ START   ☐ RECOVERY

☐ LOCK OUT   ☐ ODOMETER READING

☐ BLOCK DRIVEWAY   ☐ ILLEGAL PARKING

SPECIAL EQUIPMENT

☐ SINGLE LINE WINCHING

☐ DUAL LINE WINCHING

☐ SNATCH BLOCKS

☐ SCOTCH BLOCKS

☐ DOLLY

☐ _____

LEFT SIDE   FRONT   BACK

RIGHT SIDE

I AUTHORIZE THE TOWING OF THE ABOVE VEHICLE

X _____

CAR WAS TOWED:	DISTANCE TOWED:	
FROM:	MILEAGE END	
TO:	MILEAGE START	
	TOTAL DISTANCE TOWED	
MEMBER # _____	MILEAGE CHARGE	
P.O.# _____	TOWING CHARGE	
REMARKS _____	LABOR CHARGE	
_____	STORAGE CHARGE	
_____	TOLLS	
VEHICLE RELEASED TO _____	TAX	
WITH NO FURTHER RECOURSE TO _____	TOTAL	

TOWING INVOICE

COMPANY NAME	**24 HOUR TOWING SERVICE** **FLATBED SERVICE**	
	REQ. BY:	
(STAMP)		
NAME	DATE	
ADDRESS	TIME	
CITY	STATE	ZIP	PHONE
YEAR	MAKE / MODEL / COLOR	DRIVER
STATE	LIC NO.	VEHICLE ID NO.	

☐ SLING/HOIST   ☐ FLAT TIRE   **SPECIAL EQUIPMENT**
☐ WHEEL LIFT   ☐ OUT OF GAS   ☐ SINGLE LINE WINCHING
☐ FLAT BED/RAMP   ☐ WRECK   ☐ DUAL LINE WINCHING
☐ START   ☐ RECOVERY   ☐ SNATCH BLOCKS
☐ LOCK OUT   ☐ ODOMETER READING   ☐ SCOTCH BLOCKS
☐ BLOCK DRIVEWAY   ☐ ILLEGAL PARKING   ☐ DOLLY
    ☐ _____

LEFT SIDE   FRONT   BACK

RIGHT SIDE

I AUTHORIZE THE TOWING OF
THE ABOVE VEHICLE

X _____

CAR WAS TOWED:	**DISTANCE TOWED:**	
FROM:	MILEAGE END	
TO:	MILEAGE START	
	TOTAL DISTANCE TOWED	
MEMBER # _____	MILEAGE CHARGE	
P.O.# _____	TOWING CHARGE	
REMARKS _____	LABOR CHARGE	
_____	STORAGE CHARGE	
_____	TOLLS	
VEHICLE RELEASED TO _____	TAX	
WITH NO FURTHER RECOURSE TO _____		
	TOTAL	

TOWING INVOICE

COMPANY NAME		**24 HOUR TOWING SERVICE** **FLATBED SERVICE**
	(STAMP)	REQ. BY:
NAME		DATE
ADDRESS		TIME
CITY	STATE	ZIP	PHONE
YEAR	MAKE / MODEL / COLOR	DRIVER
STATE	LIC NO.	VEHICLE ID NO.	

☐ SLING/HOIST   ☐ FLAT TIRE   **SPECIAL EQUIPMENT**
☐ WHEEL LIFT   ☐ OUT OF GAS   ☐ SINGLE LINE WINCHING
☐ FLAT BED/RAMP   ☐ WRECK   ☐ DUAL LINE WINCHING
☐ START   ☐ RECOVERY   ☐ SNATCH BLOCKS
☐ LOCK OUT   ☐ ODOMETER READING   ☐ SCOTCH BLOCKS
☐ BLOCK DRIVEWAY   ☐ ILLEGAL PARKING   ☐ DOLLY
                                              ☐ _____

LEFT SIDE   FRONT   BACK

RIGHT SIDE

I AUTHORIZE THE TOWING OF THE ABOVE VEHICLE

X _____

CAR WAS TOWED:	**DISTANCE TOWED:**	
FROM:	MILEAGE END	
TO:	MILEAGE START	
	TOTAL DISTANCE TOWED	
MEMBER # _____	MILEAGE CHARGE	
P.O.# _____	TOWING CHARGE	
REMARKS _____	LABOR CHARGE	
_____	STORAGE CHARGE	
_____	TOLLS	
VEHICLE RELEASED TO _____	TAX	
WITH NO FURTHER RECOURSE TO _____	**TOTAL**	

TOWING INVOICE

COMPANY NAME		24 HOUR TOWING SERVICE FLATBED SERVICE	
	(STAMP)	REQ. BY:	
NAME		DATE	
ADDRESS		TIME	
CITY	STATE / ZIP	PHONE	
YEAR / MAKE / MODEL / COLOR		DRIVER	
STATE / LIC NO. / VEHICLE ID NO.			

☐ SLING/HOIST   ☐ FLAT TIRE   **SPECIAL EQUIPMENT**
☐ WHEEL LIFT   ☐ OUT OF GAS   ☐ SINGLE LINE WINCHING
☐ FLAT BED/RAMP   ☐ WRECK   ☐ DUAL LINE WINCHING
☐ START   ☐ RECOVERY   ☐ SNATCH BLOCKS
☐ LOCK OUT   ☐ ODOMETER READING   ☐ SCOTCH BLOCKS
☐ BLOCK DRIVEWAY   ☐ ILLEGAL PARKING   ☐ DOLLY
    ☐ _____

LEFT SIDE   FRONT   BACK

RIGHT SIDE

I AUTHORIZE THE TOWING OF THE ABOVE VEHICLE

X _____

CAR WAS TOWED:	DISTANCE TOWED:	
FROM:	MILEAGE END	
TO:	MILEAGE START	
	TOTAL DISTANCE TOWED	
MEMBER # _____	MILEAGE CHARGE	
P.O.# _____	TOWING CHARGE	
REMARKS _____	LABOR CHARGE	
_____	STORAGE CHARGE	
_____	TOLLS	
VEHICLE RELEASED TO _____	TAX	
WITH NO FURTHER RECOURSE TO _____	TOTAL	

TOWING INVOICE

COMPANY NAME		24 HOUR TOWING SERVICE FLATBED SERVICE	
		REQ. BY:	
	(STAMP)		
NAME		DATE	
ADDRESS		TIME	
CITY	STATE	ZIP	PHONE
YEAR	MAKE / MODEL / COLOR		DRIVER
STATE	LIC NO.	VEHICLE ID NO.	

☐ SLING/HOIST   ☐ FLAT TIRE   **SPECIAL EQUIPMENT**

☐ WHEEL LIFT   ☐ OUT OF GAS   ☐ SINGLE LINE WINCHING

☐ FLAT BED/RAMP   ☐ WRECK   ☐ DUAL LINE WINCHING

☐ START   ☐ RECOVERY   ☐ SNATCH BLOCKS

☐ LOCK OUT   ☐ ODOMETER READING   ☐ SCOTCH BLOCKS

☐ BLOCK DRIVEWAY   ☐ ILLEGAL PARKING   ☐ DOLLY

☐ _____

LEFT SIDE   FRONT   BACK

RIGHT SIDE

I AUTHORIZE THE TOWING OF THE ABOVE VEHICLE

X _____

CAR WAS TOWED:	DISTANCE TOWED:	
FROM:	MILEAGE END	
TO:	MILEAGE START	
	TOTAL DISTANCE TOWED	
MEMBER # _____	MILEAGE CHARGE	
P.O.# _____	TOWING CHARGE	
REMARKS _____	LABOR CHARGE	
_____	STORAGE CHARGE	
_____	TOLLS	
VEHICLE RELEASED TO _____	TAX	
WITH NO FURTHER RECOURSE TO _____	TOTAL	

TOWING INVOICE

COMPANY NAME				24 HOUR TOWING SERVICE FLATBED SERVICE	
			(STAMP)	REQ. BY:	
NAME				DATE	
ADDRESS				TIME	
CITY		STATE	ZIP	PHONE	
YEAR	MAKE / MODEL / COLOR			DRIVER	
STATE	LIC NO.	VEHICLE ID NO.			

☐ SLING/HOIST   ☐ FLAT TIRE   <u>SPECIAL EQUIPMENT</u>
☐ WHEEL LIFT   ☐ OUT OF GAS   ☐ SINGLE LINE WINCHING
☐ FLAT BED/RAMP   ☐ WRECK   ☐ DUAL LINE WINCHING
☐ START   ☐ RECOVERY   ☐ SNATCH BLOCKS
☐ LOCK OUT   ☐ ODOMETER READING   ☐ SCOTCH BLOCKS
☐ BLOCK DRIVEWAY   ☐ ILLEGAL PARKING   ☐ DOLLY
                                            ☐ _____

LEFT SIDE   FRONT   BACK

RIGHT SIDE

I AUTHORIZE THE TOWING OF
THE ABOVE VEHICLE

X _____

CAR WAS TOWED:		DISTANCE TOWED:	
FROM:		MILEAGE END	
TO:		MILEAGE START	
		TOTAL DISTANCE TOWED	
MEMBER # _____		MILEAGE CHARGE	
P.O.# _____		TOWING CHARGE	
REMARKS _____		LABOR CHARGE	
_____		STORAGE CHARGE	
_____		TOLLS	
VEHICLE RELEASED TO _____		TAX	
WITH NO FURTHER RECOURSE TO _____		TOTAL	

TOWING INVOICE

COMPANY NAME	24 HOUR TOWING SERVICE FLATBED SERVICE
(STAMP)	REQ. BY:
NAME	DATE
ADDRESS	TIME

CITY	STATE	ZIP	PHONE

YEAR	MAKE / MODEL / COLOR	DRIVER

STATE	LIC NO.	VEHICLE ID NO.	

□ SLING/HOIST   □ FLAT TIRE

□ WHEEL LIFT   □ OUT OF GAS

□ FLAT BED/RAMP   □ WRECK

□ START   □ RECOVERY

□ LOCK OUT   □ ODOMETER READING

□ BLOCK DRIVEWAY   □ ILLEGAL PARKING

SPECIAL EQUIPMENT

□ SINGLE LINE WINCHING

□ DUAL LINE WINCHING

□ SNATCH BLOCKS

□ SCOTCH BLOCKS

□ DOLLY

□ _____

LEFT SIDE

FRONT

BACK

RIGHT SIDE

I AUTHORIZE THE TOWING OF THE ABOVE VEHICLE

X _____

CAR WAS TOWED:	DISTANCE TOWED:	
FROM:	MILEAGE END	
TO:	MILEAGE START	
	TOTAL DISTANCE TOWED	
MEMBER # _____	MILEAGE CHARGE	
P.O.# _____	TOWING CHARGE	
REMARKS _____	LABOR CHARGE	
_____	STORAGE CHARGE	
_____	TOLLS	
VEHICLE RELEASED TO _____	TAX	
WITH NO FURTHER RECOURSE TO _____	TOTAL	

TOWING INVOICE

COMPANY NAME		24 HOUR TOWING SERVICE FLATBED SERVICE	
		REQ. BY:	
	(STAMP)		
NAME		DATE	
ADDRESS		TIME	
CITY	STATE	ZIP	PHONE
YEAR	MAKE / MODEL / COLOR		DRIVER
STATE	LIC NO.	VEHICLE ID NO.	

☐ SLING/HOIST   ☐ FLAT TIRE   **SPECIAL EQUIPMENT**
☐ WHEEL LIFT   ☐ OUT OF GAS   ☐ SINGLE LINE WINCHING
☐ FLAT BED/RAMP   ☐ WRECK   ☐ DUAL LINE WINCHING
☐ START   ☐ RECOVERY   ☐ SNATCH BLOCKS
☐ LOCK OUT   ☐ ODOMETER READING   ☐ SCOTCH BLOCKS
☐ BLOCK DRIVEWAY   ☐ ILLEGAL PARKING   ☐ DOLLY
   ☐ _____

LEFT SIDE   FRONT   BACK

RIGHT SIDE

I AUTHORIZE THE TOWING OF THE ABOVE VEHICLE

X _____

CAR WAS TOWED:	DISTANCE TOWED:	
FROM:	MILEAGE END	
TO:	MILEAGE START	
	TOTAL DISTANCE TOWED	
MEMBER # _____	MILEAGE CHARGE	
P.O.# _____	TOWING CHARGE	
REMARKS _____	LABOR CHARGE	
_____	STORAGE CHARGE	
_____		
VEHICLE RELEASED TO _____	TOLLS	
WITH NO FURTHER RECOURSE TO _____	TAX	
	TOTAL	

TOWING INVOICE

COMPANY NAME	24 HOUR TOWING SERVICE FLATBED SERVICE	
	REQ. BY:	
(STAMP)		
NAME	DATE	
ADDRESS	TIME	
CITY	STATE	ZIP	PHONE
YEAR	MAKE / MODEL / COLOR	DRIVER
STATE	LIC NO.	VEHICLE ID NO.	

☐ SLING/HOIST   ☐ FLAT TIRE   **SPECIAL EQUIPMENT**
☐ WHEEL LIFT   ☐ OUT OF GAS   ☐ SINGLE LINE WINCHING
☐ FLAT BED/RAMP   ☐ WRECK   ☐ DUAL LINE WINCHING
☐ START   ☐ RECOVERY   ☐ SNATCH BLOCKS
☐ LOCK OUT   ☐ ODOMETER READING   ☐ SCOTCH BLOCKS
☐ BLOCK DRIVEWAY   ☐ ILLEGAL PARKING   ☐ DOLLY
    ☐ _____

LEFT SIDE   FRONT   BACK

RIGHT SIDE

I AUTHORIZE THE TOWING OF THE ABOVE VEHICLE

X _____

CAR WAS TOWED:	DISTANCE TOWED:	
FROM:	MILEAGE END	
TO:	MILEAGE START	
	TOTAL DISTANCE TOWED	
MEMBER # _____	MILEAGE CHARGE	
P.O.# _____	TOWING CHARGE	
REMARKS _____	LABOR CHARGE	
_____	STORAGE CHARGE	
_____	TOLLS	
VEHICLE RELEASED TO _____	TAX	
WITH NO FURTHER RECOURSE TO _____	**TOTAL**	

TOWING INVOICE

COMPANY NAME		**24 HOUR TOWING SERVICE** **FLATBED SERVICE**
	(STAMP)	REQ. BY:
NAME		DATE
ADDRESS		TIME
CITY	STATE / ZIP	PHONE
YEAR / MAKE / MODEL / COLOR		DRIVER
STATE / LIC NO. / VEHICLE ID NO.		

☐ SLING/HOIST   ☐ FLAT TIRE   <u>SPECIAL EQUIPMENT</u>
☐ WHEEL LIFT   ☐ OUT OF GAS   ☐ SINGLE LINE WINCHING
☐ FLAT BED/RAMP   ☐ WRECK   ☐ DUAL LINE WINCHING
☐ START   ☐ RECOVERY   ☐ SNATCH BLOCKS
☐ LOCK OUT   ☐ ODOMETER READING   ☐ SCOTCH BLOCKS
☐ BLOCK DRIVEWAY   ☐ ILLEGAL PARKING   ☐ DOLLY
    ☐ _____

LEFT SIDE

FRONT   BACK

RIGHT SIDE

I AUTHORIZE THE TOWING OF THE ABOVE VEHICLE

X _____

CAR WAS TOWED:	DISTANCE TOWED:	
FROM:	MILEAGE END	
TO:	MILEAGE START	
	TOTAL DISTANCE TOWED	
MEMBER # _____	MILEAGE CHARGE	
P.O.# _____	TOWING CHARGE	
REMARKS _____	LABOR CHARGE	
_____	STORAGE CHARGE	
_____	TOLLS	
VEHICLE RELEASED TO _____	TAX	
WITH NO FURTHER RECOURSE TO _____	**TOTAL**	

TOWING INVOICE

COMPANY NAME	**24 HOUR TOWING SERVICE** **FLATBED SERVICE**
	REQ. BY:
(STAMP)	
NAME	DATE
ADDRESS	TIME
CITY	STATE	ZIP	PHONE
YEAR	MAKE / MODEL / COLOR	DRIVER
STATE	LIC NO.	VEHICLE ID NO.	

☐ SLING/HOIST　　☐ FLAT TIRE　　**SPECIAL EQUIPMENT**
☐ WHEEL LIFT　　☐ OUT OF GAS　　☐ SINGLE LINE WINCHING
☐ FLAT BED/RAMP　☐ WRECK　　　☐ DUAL LINE WINCHING
☐ START　　　　 ☐ RECOVERY　　☐ SNATCH BLOCKS
☐ LOCK OUT　　　☐ ODOMETER READING　☐ SCOTCH BLOCKS
☐ BLOCK DRIVEWAY ☐ ILLEGAL PARKING　☐ DOLLY
　　　　　　　　　　　　　　　　☐ _____

LEFT SIDE　　　　　　FRONT　　　BACK

RIGHT SIDE

I AUTHORIZE THE TOWING OF
THE ABOVE VEHICLE

X _____

CAR WAS TOWED:	DISTANCE TOWED:	
FROM:	MILEAGE END	
TO:	MILEAGE START	
	TOTAL DISTANCE TOWED	
MEMBER # _____	MILEAGE CHARGE	
P.O.# _____	TOWING CHARGE	
REMARKS _____	LABOR CHARGE	
_____	STORAGE CHARGE	
_____	TOLLS	
VEHICLE RELEASED TO _____	TAX	
WITH NO FURTHER RECOURSE TO _____	**TOTAL**	

TOWING INVOICE

COMPANY NAME	24 HOUR TOWING SERVICE FLATBED SERVICE
(STAMP)	REQ. BY:

NAME	DATE

ADDRESS	TIME

CITY	STATE	ZIP	PHONE

YEAR	MAKE / MODEL / COLOR	DRIVER

STATE	LIC NO.	VEHICLE ID NO.

☐ SLING/HOIST   ☐ FLAT TIRE

☐ WHEEL LIFT   ☐ OUT OF GAS

☐ FLAT BED/RAMP   ☐ WRECK

☐ START   ☐ RECOVERY

☐ LOCK OUT   ☐ ODOMETER READING

☐ BLOCK DRIVEWAY   ☐ ILLEGAL PARKING

SPECIAL EQUIPMENT

☐ SINGLE LINE WINCHING

☐ DUAL LINE WINCHING

☐ SNATCH BLOCKS

☐ SCOTCH BLOCKS

☐ DOLLY

☐ _____

LEFT SIDE

FRONT

BACK

RIGHT SIDE

I AUTHORIZE THE TOWING OF THE ABOVE VEHICLE

X _____

CAR WAS TOWED:	DISTANCE TOWED:	
FROM:	MILEAGE END	
TO:	MILEAGE START	
	TOTAL DISTANCE TOWED	
MEMBER # _____	MILEAGE CHARGE	
P.O.# _____	TOWING CHARGE	
REMARKS _____	LABOR CHARGE	
_____	STORAGE CHARGE	
_____	TOLLS	
VEHICLE RELEASED TO _____		
WITH NO FURTHER RECOURSE TO _____	TAX	
	TOTAL	

TOWING INVOICE

COMPANY NAME				**24 HOUR TOWING SERVICE** **FLATBED SERVICE**	
			(STAMP)	REQ. BY:	
NAME				DATE	
ADDRESS				TIME	
CITY		STATE	ZIP	PHONE	
YEAR	MAKE / MODEL / COLOR			DRIVER	
STATE	LIC NO.		VEHICLE ID NO.		

☐ SLING/HOIST ☐ FLAT TIRE **SPECIAL EQUIPMENT**
☐ WHEEL LIFT ☐ OUT OF GAS ☐ SINGLE LINE WINCHING
☐ FLAT BED/RAMP ☐ WRECK ☐ DUAL LINE WINCHING
☐ START ☐ RECOVERY ☐ SNATCH BLOCKS
☐ LOCK OUT ☐ ODOMETER READING ☐ SCOTCH BLOCKS
☐ BLOCK DRIVEWAY ☐ ILLEGAL PARKING ☐ DOLLY
☐ _____

LEFT SIDE   FRONT   BACK

RIGHT SIDE

I AUTHORIZE THE TOWING OF THE ABOVE VEHICLE

X _____

CAR WAS TOWED:	DISTANCE TOWED:	
FROM:	MILEAGE END	
TO:	MILEAGE START	
	TOTAL DISTANCE TOWED	
MEMBER # _____	MILEAGE CHARGE	
P.O.# _____	TOWING CHARGE	
REMARKS _____	LABOR CHARGE	
_____	STORAGE CHARGE	
VEHICLE RELEASED TO _____	TOLLS	
WITH NO FURTHER RECOURSE TO _____	TAX	
	TOTAL	

TOWING INVOICE

COMPANY NAME		**24 HOUR TOWING SERVICE**
		FLATBED SERVICE
	(STAMP)	REQ. BY:
NAME		DATE
ADDRESS		TIME
CITY	STATE	ZIP	PHONE
YEAR	MAKE / MODEL / COLOR	DRIVER
STATE	LIC NO.	VEHICLE ID NO.	

☐ SLING/HOIST   ☐ FLAT TIRE   **SPECIAL EQUIPMENT**
☐ WHEEL LIFT   ☐ OUT OF GAS   ☐ SINGLE LINE WINCHING
☐ FLAT BED/RAMP   ☐ WRECK   ☐ DUAL LINE WINCHING
☐ START   ☐ RECOVERY   ☐ SNATCH BLOCKS
☐ LOCK OUT   ☐ ODOMETER READING   ☐ SCOTCH BLOCKS
☐ BLOCK DRIVEWAY   ☐ ILLEGAL PARKING   ☐ DOLLY
   ☐ _____

LEFT SIDE   FRONT   BACK

RIGHT SIDE

I AUTHORIZE THE TOWING OF THE ABOVE VEHICLE

X _____

CAR WAS TOWED:	DISTANCE TOWED:	
FROM:	MILEAGE END	
TO:	MILEAGE START	
	TOTAL DISTANCE TOWED	
MEMBER # _____	MILEAGE CHARGE	
P.O.# _____	TOWING CHARGE	
REMARKS _____	LABOR CHARGE	
_____	STORAGE CHARGE	
_____	TOLLS	
VEHICLE RELEASED TO _____	TAX	
WITH NO FURTHER RECOURSE TO _____	**TOTAL**	

TOWING INVOICE

COMPANY NAME		24 HOUR TOWING SERVICE FLATBED SERVICE	
	(STAMP)	REQ. BY:	
NAME		DATE	
ADDRESS		TIME	
CITY	STATE	ZIP	PHONE
YEAR	MAKE / MODEL / COLOR	DRIVER	
STATE	LIC NO.	VEHICLE ID NO.	

☐ SLING/HOIST   ☐ FLAT TIRE   **SPECIAL EQUIPMENT**
☐ WHEEL LIFT   ☐ OUT OF GAS   ☐ SINGLE LINE WINCHING
☐ FLAT BED/RAMP   ☐ WRECK   ☐ DUAL LINE WINCHING
☐ START   ☐ RECOVERY   ☐ SNATCH BLOCKS
☐ LOCK OUT   ☐ ODOMETER READING   ☐ SCOTCH BLOCKS
☐ BLOCK DRIVEWAY   ☐ ILLEGAL PARKING   ☐ DOLLY
    ☐ _____

LEFT SIDE   FRONT   BACK

RIGHT SIDE

I AUTHORIZE THE TOWING OF THE ABOVE VEHICLE

X _____

CAR WAS TOWED:	DISTANCE TOWED:	
FROM:	MILEAGE END	
TO:	MILEAGE START	
	TOTAL DISTANCE TOWED	
MEMBER # _____	MILEAGE CHARGE	
P.O.# _____	TOWING CHARGE	
REMARKS _____	LABOR CHARGE	
_____	STORAGE CHARGE	
_____	TOLLS	
VEHICLE RELEASED TO _____	TAX	
WITH NO FURTHER RECOURSE TO _____	**TOTAL**	

TOWING INVOICE

COMPANY NAME	24 HOUR TOWING SERVICE FLATBED SERVICE
(STAMP)	REQ. BY:

NAME	DATE

ADDRESS	TIME

CITY	STATE	ZIP	PHONE

YEAR	MAKE / MODEL / COLOR	DRIVER

STATE	LIC NO.	VEHICLE ID NO.	

- ☐ SLING/HOIST
- ☐ WHEEL LIFT
- ☐ FLAT BED/RAMP
- ☐ START
- ☐ LOCK OUT
- ☐ BLOCK DRIVEWAY

- ☐ FLAT TIRE
- ☐ OUT OF GAS
- ☐ WRECK
- ☐ RECOVERY
- ☐ ODOMETER READING
- ☐ ILLEGAL PARKING

SPECIAL EQUIPMENT
- ☐ SINGLE LINE WINCHING
- ☐ DUAL LINE WINCHING
- ☐ SNATCH BLOCKS
- ☐ SCOTCH BLOCKS
- ☐ DOLLY
- ☐ _____

LEFT SIDE

FRONT

BACK

RIGHT SIDE

I AUTHORIZE THE TOWING OF THE ABOVE VEHICLE

X _____

CAR WAS TOWED: | **DISTANCE TOWED:**

FROM:

TO:

MEMBER # _____

P.O.# _____

REMARKS _____

_____

_____

VEHICLE RELEASED TO _____

WITH NO FURTHER RECOURSE TO _____

MILEAGE END	
MILEAGE START	
TOTAL DISTANCE TOWED	
MILEAGE CHARGE	
TOWING CHARGE	
LABOR CHARGE	
STORAGE CHARGE	
TOLLS	
TAX	
TOTAL	

TOWING INVOICE

COMPANY NAME	**24 HOUR TOWING SERVICE FLATBED SERVICE**	
	REQ. BY:	
(STAMP)		
NAME	DATE	
ADDRESS	TIME	
CITY / STATE / ZIP	PHONE	
YEAR / MAKE / MODEL / COLOR	DRIVER	
STATE / LIC NO. / VEHICLE ID NO.		

☐ SLING/HOIST ☐ FLAT TIRE

☐ WHEEL LIFT ☐ OUT OF GAS

☐ FLAT BED/RAMP ☐ WRECK

☐ START ☐ RECOVERY

☐ LOCK OUT ☐ ODOMETER READING

☐ BLOCK DRIVEWAY ☐ ILLEGAL PARKING

SPECIAL EQUIPMENT

☐ SINGLE LINE WINCHING

☐ DUAL LINE WINCHING

☐ SNATCH BLOCKS

☐ SCOTCH BLOCKS

☐ DOLLY

☐ _____

LEFT SIDE

FRONT

BACK

RIGHT SIDE

I AUTHORIZE THE TOWING OF THE ABOVE VEHICLE

X _____

CAR WAS TOWED:

FROM:

TO:

MEMBER # _____

P.O.# _____

REMARKS _____

_____

_____

VEHICLE RELEASED TO _____
WITH NO FURTHER RECOURSE TO _____

DISTANCE TOWED:

MILEAGE END	
MILEAGE START	
TOTAL DISTANCE TOWED	
MILEAGE CHARGE	
TOWING CHARGE	
LABOR CHARGE	
STORAGE CHARGE	
TOLLS	
TAX	
TOTAL	

TOWING INVOICE

COMPANY NAME		**24 HOUR TOWING SERVICE** **FLATBED SERVICE**
	(STAMP)	REQ. BY:
NAME		DATE
ADDRESS		TIME
CITY	STATE / ZIP	PHONE
YEAR / MAKE / MODEL / COLOR		DRIVER
STATE / LIC NO. / VEHICLE ID NO.		

☐ SLING/HOIST ☐ FLAT TIRE

☐ WHEEL LIFT ☐ OUT OF GAS

☐ FLAT BED/RAMP ☐ WRECK

☐ START ☐ RECOVERY

☐ LOCK OUT ☐ ODOMETER READING

☐ BLOCK DRIVEWAY ☐ ILLEGAL PARKING

SPECIAL EQUIPMENT

☐ SINGLE LINE WINCHING

☐ DUAL LINE WINCHING

☐ SNATCH BLOCKS

☐ SCOTCH BLOCKS

☐ DOLLY

☐ _____

LEFT SIDE

FRONT

BACK

RIGHT SIDE

I AUTHORIZE THE TOWING OF THE ABOVE VEHICLE

X _____

CAR WAS TOWED:	DISTANCE TOWED:	
FROM:	MILEAGE END	
TO:	MILEAGE START	
	TOTAL DISTANCE TOWED	
MEMBER # _____	MILEAGE CHARGE	
P.O.# _____	TOWING CHARGE	
REMARKS _____	LABOR CHARGE	
_____	STORAGE CHARGE	
_____	TOLLS	
VEHICLE RELEASED TO _____	TAX	
WITH NO FURTHER RECOURSE TO _____	**TOTAL**	

TOWING INVOICE

COMPANY NAME		24 HOUR TOWING SERVICE FLATBED SERVICE	
	(STAMP)	REQ. BY:	
NAME		DATE	
ADDRESS		TIME	
CITY	STATE ZIP	PHONE	
YEAR	MAKE / MODEL / COLOR	DRIVER	
STATE	LIC NO.	VEHICLE ID NO.	

☐ SLING/HOIST   ☐ FLAT TIRE   **SPECIAL EQUIPMENT**
☐ WHEEL LIFT   ☐ OUT OF GAS   ☐ SINGLE LINE WINCHING
☐ FLAT BED/RAMP   ☐ WRECK   ☐ DUAL LINE WINCHING
☐ START   ☐ RECOVERY   ☐ SNATCH BLOCKS
☐ LOCK OUT   ☐ ODOMETER READING   ☐ SCOTCH BLOCKS
☐ BLOCK DRIVEWAY   ☐ ILLEGAL PARKING   ☐ DOLLY
    ☐ _____

LEFT SIDE   FRONT   BACK

RIGHT SIDE

I AUTHORIZE THE TOWING OF THE ABOVE VEHICLE

X _____

CAR WAS TOWED:

	DISTANCE TOWED:	
FROM:	MILEAGE END	
TO:	MILEAGE START	
	TOTAL DISTANCE TOWED	
MEMBER # _____	MILEAGE CHARGE	
P.O.# _____	TOWING CHARGE	
REMARKS _____	LABOR CHARGE	
_____	STORAGE CHARGE	
_____		
VEHICLE RELEASED TO _____	TOLLS	
WITH NO FURTHER RECOURSE TO _____	TAX	
	TOTAL	

TOWING INVOICE

COMPANY NAME		24 HOUR TOWING SERVICE FLATBED SERVICE	
	(STAMP)	REQ. BY:	
NAME		DATE	
ADDRESS		TIME	
CITY	STATE	ZIP	PHONE
YEAR	MAKE / MODEL / COLOR		DRIVER
STATE	LIC NO.	VEHICLE ID NO.	

☐ SLING/HOIST   ☐ FLAT TIRE   **SPECIAL EQUIPMENT**
☐ WHEEL LIFT   ☐ OUT OF GAS   ☐ SINGLE LINE WINCHING
☐ FLAT BED/RAMP   ☐ WRECK   ☐ DUAL LINE WINCHING
☐ START   ☐ RECOVERY   ☐ SNATCH BLOCKS
☐ LOCK OUT   ☐ ODOMETER READING   ☐ SCOTCH BLOCKS
☐ BLOCK DRIVEWAY   ☐ ILLEGAL PARKING   ☐ DOLLY
    ☐ _____

LEFT SIDE   FRONT   BACK

RIGHT SIDE

I AUTHORIZE THE TOWING OF THE ABOVE VEHICLE

X _____

CAR WAS TOWED:		DISTANCE TOWED:	
FROM:		MILEAGE END	
TO:		MILEAGE START	
		TOTAL DISTANCE TOWED	
MEMBER # _____		MILEAGE CHARGE	
P.O.# _____		TOWING CHARGE	
REMARKS _____		LABOR CHARGE	
_____		STORAGE CHARGE	
_____		TOLLS	
VEHICLE RELEASED TO _____		TAX	
WITH NO FURTHER RECOURSE TO _____		TOTAL	

TOWING INVOICE

COMPANY NAME		24 HOUR TOWING SERVICE FLATBED SERVICE	
	(STAMP)	REQ. BY:	
NAME		DATE	
ADDRESS		TIME	
CITY	STATE	ZIP	PHONE
YEAR	MAKE / MODEL / COLOR		DRIVER
STATE	LIC NO.	VEHICLE ID NO.	

☐ SLING/HOIST ☐ FLAT TIRE **SPECIAL EQUIPMENT**
☐ WHEEL LIFT ☐ OUT OF GAS ☐ SINGLE LINE WINCHING
☐ FLAT BED/RAMP ☐ WRECK ☐ DUAL LINE WINCHING
☐ START ☐ RECOVERY ☐ SNATCH BLOCKS
☐ LOCK OUT ☐ ODOMETER READING ☐ SCOTCH BLOCKS
☐ BLOCK DRIVEWAY ☐ ILLEGAL PARKING ☐ DOLLY
☐ _____

LEFT SIDE   FRONT   BACK

RIGHT SIDE

I AUTHORIZE THE TOWING OF
THE ABOVE VEHICLE

X _____

CAR WAS TOWED:	DISTANCE TOWED:	
FROM:	MILEAGE END	
TO:	MILEAGE START	
	TOTAL DISTANCE TOWED	
MEMBER # _____	MILEAGE CHARGE	
P.O.# _____	TOWING CHARGE	
REMARKS _____	LABOR CHARGE	
_____	STORAGE CHARGE	
VEHICLE RELEASED TO _____	TOLLS	
WITH NO FURTHER RECOURSE TO _____	TAX	
	TOTAL	

TOWING INVOICE

COMPANY NAME		24 HOUR TOWING SERVICE FLATBED SERVICE	
	(STAMP)	REQ. BY:	
NAME		DATE	
ADDRESS		TIME	
CITY	STATE	ZIP	PHONE
YEAR	MAKE / MODEL / COLOR		DRIVER
STATE	LIC NO.	VEHICLE ID NO.	

- ☐ SLING/HOIST
- ☐ WHEEL LIFT
- ☐ FLAT BED/RAMP
- ☐ START
- ☐ LOCK OUT
- ☐ BLOCK DRIVEWAY

- ☐ FLAT TIRE
- ☐ OUT OF GAS
- ☐ WRECK
- ☐ RECOVERY
- ☐ ODOMETER READING
- ☐ ILLEGAL PARKING

SPECIAL EQUIPMENT
- ☐ SINGLE LINE WINCHING
- ☐ DUAL LINE WINCHING
- ☐ SNATCH BLOCKS
- ☐ SCOTCH BLOCKS
- ☐ DOLLY
- ☐ _____

LEFT SIDE   FRONT   BACK

RIGHT SIDE

I AUTHORIZE THE TOWING OF
THE ABOVE VEHICLE

X _____

CAR WAS TOWED:	DISTANCE TOWED:	
FROM:	MILEAGE END	
TO:	MILEAGE START	
	TOTAL DISTANCE TOWED	
MEMBER # _____	MILEAGE CHARGE	
P.O.# _____	TOWING CHARGE	
REMARKS _____	LABOR CHARGE	
_____	STORAGE CHARGE	
_____	TOLLS	
VEHICLE RELEASED TO _____	TAX	
WITH NO FURTHER RECOURSE TO _____	TOTAL	

TOWING INVOICE

COMPANY NAME		**24 HOUR TOWING SERVICE** **FLATBED SERVICE**
	(STAMP)	REQ. BY:
NAME		DATE
ADDRESS		TIME
CITY	STATE / ZIP	PHONE
YEAR / MAKE / MODEL / COLOR		DRIVER
STATE / LIC NO. / VEHICLE ID NO.		

☐ SLING/HOIST
☐ WHEEL LIFT
☐ FLAT BED/RAMP
☐ START
☐ LOCK OUT
☐ BLOCK DRIVEWAY

☐ FLAT TIRE
☐ OUT OF GAS
☐ WRECK
☐ RECOVERY
☐ ODOMETER READING
☐ ILLEGAL PARKING

SPECIAL EQUIPMENT
☐ SINGLE LINE WINCHING
☐ DUAL LINE WINCHING
☐ SNATCH BLOCKS
☐ SCOTCH BLOCKS
☐ DOLLY
☐ _____

LEFT SIDE

FRONT

BACK

RIGHT SIDE

I AUTHORIZE THE TOWING OF THE ABOVE VEHICLE

X _____

CAR WAS TOWED:

DISTANCE TOWED:

FROM:

TO:

MEMBER # _____

P.O.# _____

REMARKS _____

_____

_____

VEHICLE RELEASED TO _____
WITH NO FURTHER RECOURSE TO _____

MILEAGE END	
MILEAGE START	
TOTAL DISTANCE TOWED	
MILEAGE CHARGE	
TOWING CHARGE	
LABOR CHARGE	
STORAGE CHARGE	
TOLLS	
TAX	
TOTAL	

TOWING INVOICE

COMPANY NAME	24 HOUR TOWING SERVICE FLATBED SERVICE	
(STAMP)	REQ. BY:	
NAME	DATE	
ADDRESS	TIME	
CITY	STATE	ZIP	PHONE
YEAR	MAKE / MODEL / COLOR	DRIVER
STATE	LIC NO.	VEHICLE ID NO.	

☐ SLING/HOIST   ☐ FLAT TIRE   **SPECIAL EQUIPMENT**
☐ WHEEL LIFT   ☐ OUT OF GAS   ☐ SINGLE LINE WINCHING
☐ FLAT BED/RAMP   ☐ WRECK   ☐ DUAL LINE WINCHING
☐ START   ☐ RECOVERY   ☐ SNATCH BLOCKS
☐ LOCK OUT   ☐ ODOMETER READING   ☐ SCOTCH BLOCKS
☐ BLOCK DRIVEWAY   ☐ ILLEGAL PARKING   ☐ DOLLY
☐ _____

LEFT SIDE   FRONT   BACK

RIGHT SIDE

I AUTHORIZE THE TOWING OF THE ABOVE VEHICLE

X _____

CAR WAS TOWED:	DISTANCE TOWED:	
FROM:	MILEAGE END	
TO:	MILEAGE START	
	TOTAL DISTANCE TOWED	
MEMBER # _____	MILEAGE CHARGE	
P.O.# _____	TOWING CHARGE	
REMARKS _____	LABOR CHARGE	
_____	STORAGE CHARGE	
VEHICLE RELEASED TO _____	TOLLS	
WITH NO FURTHER RECOURSE TO _____	TAX	
	TOTAL	

TOWING INVOICE

COMPANY NAME	**24 HOUR TOWING SERVICE** **FLATBED SERVICE**
(STAMP)	REQ. BY:
NAME	DATE
ADDRESS	TIME

CITY		STATE	ZIP	PHONE
YEAR	MAKE / MODEL / COLOR			DRIVER
STATE	LIC NO.	VEHICLE ID NO.		

☐ SLING/HOIST   ☐ FLAT TIRE   **SPECIAL EQUIPMENT**
☐ WHEEL LIFT   ☐ OUT OF GAS   ☐ SINGLE LINE WINCHING
☐ FLAT BED/RAMP   ☐ WRECK   ☐ DUAL LINE WINCHING
☐ START   ☐ RECOVERY   ☐ SNATCH BLOCKS
☐ LOCK OUT   ☐ ODOMETER READING   ☐ SCOTCH BLOCKS
☐ BLOCK DRIVEWAY   ☐ ILLEGAL PARKING   ☐ DOLLY
    ☐ _____

LEFT SIDE   FRONT   BACK

RIGHT SIDE

I AUTHORIZE THE TOWING OF THE ABOVE VEHICLE

X _____

CAR WAS TOWED:	DISTANCE TOWED:	
FROM:	MILEAGE END	
TO:	MILEAGE START	
	TOTAL DISTANCE TOWED	
MEMBER # _____	MILEAGE CHARGE	
P.O.# _____	TOWING CHARGE	
REMARKS _____	LABOR CHARGE	
_____	STORAGE CHARGE	
_____	TOLLS	
VEHICLE RELEASED TO _____	TAX	
WITH NO FURTHER RECOURSE TO _____	**TOTAL**	

TOWING INVOICE

COMPANY NAME				24 HOUR TOWING SERVICE FLATBED SERVICE	
			(STAMP)	REQ. BY:	
NAME				DATE	
ADDRESS				TIME	
CITY		STATE	ZIP	PHONE	
YEAR	MAKE / MODEL / COLOR			DRIVER	
STATE	LIC NO.	VEHICLE ID NO.			

☐ SLING/HOIST   ☐ FLAT TIRE   **SPECIAL EQUIPMENT**
☐ WHEEL LIFT   ☐ OUT OF GAS   ☐ SINGLE LINE WINCHING
☐ FLAT BED/RAMP   ☐ WRECK   ☐ DUAL LINE WINCHING
☐ START   ☐ RECOVERY   ☐ SNATCH BLOCKS
☐ LOCK OUT   ☐ ODOMETER READING   ☐ SCOTCH BLOCKS
☐ BLOCK DRIVEWAY   ☐ ILLEGAL PARKING   ☐ DOLLY
☐ _____

LEFT SIDE   FRONT   BACK

RIGHT SIDE

I AUTHORIZE THE TOWING OF THE ABOVE VEHICLE

X _____

CAR WAS TOWED:	DISTANCE TOWED:	
FROM:	MILEAGE END	
TO:	MILEAGE START	
	TOTAL DISTANCE TOWED	
MEMBER # _____	MILEAGE CHARGE	
P.O.# _____	TOWING CHARGE	
REMARKS _____	LABOR CHARGE	
_____	STORAGE CHARGE	
_____	TOLLS	
VEHICLE RELEASED TO _____	TAX	
WITH NO FURTHER RECOURSE TO _____		
	TOTAL	

TOWING INVOICE

COMPANY NAME	24 HOUR TOWING SERVICE FLATBED SERVICE	
(STAMP)	REQ. BY:	
NAME	DATE	
ADDRESS	TIME	
CITY STATE ZIP	PHONE	
YEAR MAKE / MODEL / COLOR	DRIVER	
STATE LIC NO. VEHICLE ID NO.		

☐ SLING/HOIST   ☐ FLAT TIRE

☐ WHEEL LIFT   ☐ OUT OF GAS

☐ FLAT BED/RAMP   ☐ WRECK

☐ START   ☐ RECOVERY

☐ LOCK OUT   ☐ ODOMETER READING

☐ BLOCK DRIVEWAY   ☐ ILLEGAL PARKING

SPECIAL EQUIPMENT

☐ SINGLE LINE WINCHING

☐ DUAL LINE WINCHING

☐ SNATCH BLOCKS

☐ SCOTCH BLOCKS

☐ DOLLY

☐ _____

LEFT SIDE

FRONT

BACK

RIGHT SIDE

I AUTHORIZE THE TOWING OF THE ABOVE VEHICLE

X _____

CAR WAS TOWED:

DISTANCE TOWED:

FROM:

TO:

MEMBER # _____

P.O.# _____

REMARKS _____

_____

_____

VEHICLE RELEASED TO _____

WITH NO FURTHER RECOURSE TO _____

MILEAGE END	
MILEAGE START	
TOTAL DISTANCE TOWED	
MILEAGE CHARGE	
TOWING CHARGE	
LABOR CHARGE	
STORAGE CHARGE	
TOLLS	
TAX	
TOTAL	

TOWING INVOICE

COMPANY NAME		24 HOUR TOWING SERVICE FLATBED SERVICE	
	(STAMP)	REQ. BY:	
NAME		DATE	
ADDRESS		TIME	
CITY	STATE	ZIP	PHONE
YEAR	MAKE / MODEL / COLOR		DRIVER
STATE	LIC NO.	VEHICLE ID NO.	

- ☐ SLING/HOIST
- ☐ WHEEL LIFT
- ☐ FLAT BED/RAMP
- ☐ START
- ☐ LOCK OUT
- ☐ BLOCK DRIVEWAY

- ☐ FLAT TIRE
- ☐ OUT OF GAS
- ☐ WRECK
- ☐ RECOVERY
- ☐ ODOMETER READING
- ☐ ILLEGAL PARKING

SPECIAL EQUIPMENT
- ☐ SINGLE LINE WINCHING
- ☐ DUAL LINE WINCHING
- ☐ SNATCH BLOCKS
- ☐ SCOTCH BLOCKS
- ☐ DOLLY
- ☐ _____

LEFT SIDE   FRONT   BACK

RIGHT SIDE

I AUTHORIZE THE TOWING OF THE ABOVE VEHICLE

X _____

CAR WAS TOWED:		DISTANCE TOWED:	
FROM:		MILEAGE END	
TO:		MILEAGE START	
		TOTAL DISTANCE TOWED	
MEMBER # _____		MILEAGE CHARGE	
P.O.# _____		TOWING CHARGE	
REMARKS _____		LABOR CHARGE	
_____		STORAGE CHARGE	
_____		TOLLS	
VEHICLE RELEASED TO _____		TAX	
WITH NO FURTHER RECOURSE TO _____		TOTAL	

TOWING INVOICE

COMPANY NAME		24 HOUR TOWING SERVICE FLATBED SERVICE	
	(STAMP)	REQ. BY:	
NAME		DATE	
ADDRESS		TIME	
CITY	STATE / ZIP	PHONE	
YEAR	MAKE / MODEL / COLOR	DRIVER	
STATE	LIC NO. / VEHICLE ID NO.		

- ☐ SLING/HOIST
- ☐ WHEEL LIFT
- ☐ FLAT BED/RAMP
- ☐ START
- ☐ LOCK OUT
- ☐ BLOCK DRIVEWAY

- ☐ FLAT TIRE
- ☐ OUT OF GAS
- ☐ WRECK
- ☐ RECOVERY
- ☐ ODOMETER READING
- ☐ ILLEGAL PARKING

SPECIAL EQUIPMENT
- ☐ SINGLE LINE WINCHING
- ☐ DUAL LINE WINCHING
- ☐ SNATCH BLOCKS
- ☐ SCOTCH BLOCKS
- ☐ DOLLY
- ☐ _____

LEFT SIDE

FRONT

BACK

RIGHT SIDE

I AUTHORIZE THE TOWING OF THE ABOVE VEHICLE

X _____

CAR WAS TOWED:	DISTANCE TOWED:	
FROM:	MILEAGE END	
TO:	MILEAGE START	
	TOTAL DISTANCE TOWED	
MEMBER # _____	MILEAGE CHARGE	
P.O.# _____	TOWING CHARGE	
REMARKS _____	LABOR CHARGE	
_____	STORAGE CHARGE	
_____	TOLLS	
VEHICLE RELEASED TO _____		
WITH NO FURTHER RECOURSE TO _____	TAX	
	TOTAL	

TOWING INVOICE

COMPANY NAME		24 HOUR TOWING SERVICE FLATBED SERVICE	
	(STAMP)	**REQ. BY:**	
NAME		**DATE**	
ADDRESS		**TIME**	
CITY	**STATE**	**ZIP**	**PHONE**
YEAR	**MAKE / MODEL / COLOR**		**DRIVER**
STATE	**LIC NO.**	**VEHICLE ID NO.**	

☐ SLING/HOIST   ☐ FLAT TIRE   SPECIAL EQUIPMENT
☐ WHEEL LIFT   ☐ OUT OF GAS   ☐ SINGLE LINE WINCHING
☐ FLAT BED/RAMP   ☐ WRECK   ☐ DUAL LINE WINCHING
☐ START   ☐ RECOVERY   ☐ SNATCH BLOCKS
☐ LOCK OUT   ☐ ODOMETER READING   ☐ SCOTCH BLOCKS
☐ BLOCK DRIVEWAY   ☐ ILLEGAL PARKING   ☐ DOLLY
   ☐ _____

LEFT SIDE   FRONT   BACK

RIGHT SIDE

I AUTHORIZE THE TOWING OF THE ABOVE VEHICLE

X _____

CAR WAS TOWED:	DISTANCE TOWED:	
FROM:	**MILEAGE END**	
TO:	**MILEAGE START**	
	TOTAL DISTANCE TOWED	
MEMBER # _____	**MILEAGE CHARGE**	
P.O.# _____	**TOWING CHARGE**	
REMARKS _____	**LABOR CHARGE**	
_____	**STORAGE CHARGE**	
_____	**TOLLS**	
VEHICLE RELEASED TO _____	**TAX**	
WITH NO FURTHER RECOURSE TO _____	**TOTAL**	

TOWING INVOICE

COMPANY NAME	24 HOUR TOWING SERVICE FLATBED SERVICE	
(STAMP)	REQ. BY:	
NAME	DATE	
ADDRESS	TIME	
CITY	STATE	ZIP	PHONE
YEAR	MAKE / MODEL / COLOR	DRIVER
STATE	LIC NO.	VEHICLE ID NO.	

- ☐ SLING/HOIST
- ☐ WHEEL LIFT
- ☐ FLAT BED/RAMP
- ☐ START
- ☐ LOCK OUT
- ☐ BLOCK DRIVEWAY

- ☐ FLAT TIRE
- ☐ OUT OF GAS
- ☐ WRECK
- ☐ RECOVERY
- ☐ ODOMETER READING
- ☐ ILLEGAL PARKING

SPECIAL EQUIPMENT
- ☐ SINGLE LINE WINCHING
- ☐ DUAL LINE WINCHING
- ☐ SNATCH BLOCKS
- ☐ SCOTCH BLOCKS
- ☐ DOLLY
- ☐ _____

LEFT SIDE

FRONT

BACK

RIGHT SIDE

I AUTHORIZE THE TOWING OF THE ABOVE VEHICLE

X _____

CAR WAS TOWED:

FROM:

TO:

MEMBER # _____

P.O.# _____

REMARKS _____

_____

_____

VEHICLE RELEASED TO _____
WITH NO FURTHER RECOURSE TO _____

DISTANCE TOWED:

MILEAGE END	
MILEAGE START	
TOTAL DISTANCE TOWED	
MILEAGE CHARGE	
TOWING CHARGE	
LABOR CHARGE	
STORAGE CHARGE	
TOLLS	
TAX	
TOTAL	

TOWING INVOICE

COMPANY NAME		24 HOUR TOWING SERVICE FLATBED SERVICE	
	(STAMP)	REQ. BY:	
NAME		DATE	
ADDRESS		TIME	
CITY	STATE	ZIP	PHONE
YEAR	MAKE / MODEL / COLOR		DRIVER
STATE	LIC NO.	VEHICLE ID NO.	

☐ SLING/HOIST   ☐ FLAT TIRE   **SPECIAL EQUIPMENT**
☐ WHEEL LIFT   ☐ OUT OF GAS   ☐ SINGLE LINE WINCHING
☐ FLAT BED/RAMP   ☐ WRECK   ☐ DUAL LINE WINCHING
☐ START   ☐ RECOVERY   ☐ SNATCH BLOCKS
☐ LOCK OUT   ☐ ODOMETER READING   ☐ SCOTCH BLOCKS
☐ BLOCK DRIVEWAY   ☐ ILLEGAL PARKING   ☐ DOLLY
                                            ☐ _____

LEFT SIDE   FRONT   BACK

RIGHT SIDE

I AUTHORIZE THE TOWING OF
THE ABOVE VEHICLE

X _____

CAR WAS TOWED:	DISTANCE TOWED:	
FROM:	MILEAGE END	
TO:	MILEAGE START	
	TOTAL DISTANCE TOWED	
MEMBER # _____	MILEAGE CHARGE	
P.O.# _____	TOWING CHARGE	
REMARKS _____	LABOR CHARGE	
_____	STORAGE CHARGE	
_____	TOLLS	
VEHICLE RELEASED TO _____	TAX	
WITH NO FURTHER RECOURSE TO _____	TOTAL	

TOWING INVOICE

COMPANY NAME		24 HOUR TOWING SERVICE FLATBED SERVICE	
	(STAMP)	REQ. BY:	
NAME		DATE	
ADDRESS		TIME	
CITY	STATE	ZIP	PHONE
YEAR	MAKE / MODEL / COLOR		DRIVER
STATE	LIC NO.	VEHICLE ID NO.	

☐ SLING/HOIST   ☐ FLAT TIRE
☐ WHEEL LIFT   ☐ OUT OF GAS
☐ FLAT BED/RAMP   ☐ WRECK
☐ START   ☐ RECOVERY
☐ LOCK OUT   ☐ ODOMETER READING
☐ BLOCK DRIVEWAY   ☐ ILLEGAL PARKING

SPECIAL EQUIPMENT
☐ SINGLE LINE WINCHING
☐ DUAL LINE WINCHING
☐ SNATCH BLOCKS
☐ SCOTCH BLOCKS
☐ DOLLY
☐ _____

LEFT SIDE   FRONT   BACK

RIGHT SIDE

I AUTHORIZE THE TOWING OF THE ABOVE VEHICLE

X _____

CAR WAS TOWED:

FROM:

TO:

MEMBER # _____

P.O.# _____

REMARKS _____

_____

_____

VEHICLE RELEASED TO _____
WITH NO FURTHER RECOURSE TO _____

DISTANCE TOWED:	
MILEAGE END	
MILEAGE START	
TOTAL DISTANCE TOWED	
MILEAGE CHARGE	
TOWING CHARGE	
LABOR CHARGE	
STORAGE CHARGE	
TOLLS	
TAX	
TOTAL	

TOWING INVOICE

COMPANY NAME	24 HOUR TOWING SERVICE FLATBED SERVICE
(STAMP)	REQ. BY:

NAME	DATE
ADDRESS	TIME

CITY	STATE	ZIP	PHONE

YEAR	MAKE / MODEL / COLOR	DRIVER

STATE	LIC NO.	VEHICLE ID NO.	

☐ SLING/HOIST   ☐ FLAT TIRE   SPECIAL EQUIPMENT
☐ WHEEL LIFT   ☐ OUT OF GAS   ☐ SINGLE LINE WINCHING
☐ FLAT BED/RAMP   ☐ WRECK   ☐ DUAL LINE WINCHING
☐ START   ☐ RECOVERY   ☐ SNATCH BLOCKS
☐ LOCK OUT   ☐ ODOMETER READING   ☐ SCOTCH BLOCKS
☐ BLOCK DRIVEWAY   ☐ ILLEGAL PARKING   ☐ DOLLY
☐ _____

LEFT SIDE   FRONT   BACK

RIGHT SIDE

I AUTHORIZE THE TOWING OF THE ABOVE VEHICLE

X _____

CAR WAS TOWED: DISTANCE TOWED:

FROM:	MILEAGE END	
TO:	MILEAGE START	
	TOTAL DISTANCE TOWED	
MEMBER # _____	MILEAGE CHARGE	
P.O.# _____	TOWING CHARGE	
REMARKS _____	LABOR CHARGE	
_____	STORAGE CHARGE	
_____	TOLLS	
VEHICLE RELEASED TO _____	TAX	
WITH NO FURTHER RECOURSE TO _____	TOTAL	

TOWING INVOICE

COMPANY NAME	24 HOUR TOWING SERVICE FLATBED SERVICE

COMPANY NAME (STAMP)	**24 HOUR TOWING SERVICE** **FLATBED SERVICE**
	REQ. BY:
NAME	DATE
ADDRESS	TIME
CITY STATE ZIP	PHONE
YEAR MAKE / MODEL / COLOR	DRIVER
STATE LIC NO. VEHICLE ID NO.	

- ☐ SLING/HOIST
- ☐ WHEEL LIFT
- ☐ FLAT BED/RAMP
- ☐ START
- ☐ LOCK OUT
- ☐ BLOCK DRIVEWAY

- ☐ FLAT TIRE
- ☐ OUT OF GAS
- ☐ WRECK
- ☐ RECOVERY
- ☐ ODOMETER READING
- ☐ ILLEGAL PARKING

SPECIAL EQUIPMENT
- ☐ SINGLE LINE WINCHING
- ☐ DUAL LINE WINCHING
- ☐ SNATCH BLOCKS
- ☐ SCOTCH BLOCKS
- ☐ DOLLY
- ☐ _____

LEFT SIDE

FRONT   BACK

RIGHT SIDE

I AUTHORIZE THE TOWING OF THE ABOVE VEHICLE

X _____

CAR WAS TOWED:	DISTANCE TOWED:	
FROM:	MILEAGE END	
TO:	MILEAGE START	
	TOTAL DISTANCE TOWED	
MEMBER # _____	MILEAGE CHARGE	
P.O.# _____	TOWING CHARGE	
REMARKS _____	LABOR CHARGE	
_____	STORAGE CHARGE	
_____	TOLLS	
VEHICLE RELEASED TO _____ WITH NO FURTHER RECOURSE TO _____	TAX	
	TOTAL	

TOWING INVOICE

COMPANY NAME	**24 HOUR TOWING SERVICE FLATBED SERVICE**
(STAMP)	REQ. BY:
NAME	DATE
ADDRESS	TIME

CITY	STATE	ZIP	PHONE

YEAR	MAKE / MODEL / COLOR	DRIVER

STATE	LIC NO.	VEHICLE ID NO.

☐ SLING/HOIST   ☐ FLAT TIRE

☐ WHEEL LIFT   ☐ OUT OF GAS

☐ FLAT BED/RAMP   ☐ WRECK

☐ START   ☐ RECOVERY

☐ LOCK OUT   ☐ ODOMETER READING

☐ BLOCK DRIVEWAY   ☐ ILLEGAL PARKING

SPECIAL EQUIPMENT

☐ SINGLE LINE WINCHING

☐ DUAL LINE WINCHING

☐ SNATCH BLOCKS

☐ SCOTCH BLOCKS

☐ DOLLY

☐ _____

LEFT SIDE   FRONT   BACK

RIGHT SIDE

I AUTHORIZE THE TOWING OF THE ABOVE VEHICLE

X _____

CAR WAS TOWED:	DISTANCE TOWED:	
FROM:	MILEAGE END	
TO:	MILEAGE START	
	TOTAL DISTANCE TOWED	
MEMBER # _____	MILEAGE CHARGE	
P.O.# _____	TOWING CHARGE	
REMARKS _____	LABOR CHARGE	
_____	STORAGE CHARGE	
_____	TOLLS	
VEHICLE RELEASED TO _____	TAX	
WITH NO FURTHER RECOURSE TO _____	TOTAL	

TOWING INVOICE

COMPANY NAME	**24 HOUR TOWING SERVICE FLATBED SERVICE**
(STAMP)	REQ. BY:

NAME	DATE
ADDRESS	TIME

CITY	STATE	ZIP	PHONE
YEAR	MAKE / MODEL / COLOR		DRIVER
STATE	LIC NO.	VEHICLE ID NO.	

☐ SLING/HOIST   ☐ FLAT TIRE   **SPECIAL EQUIPMENT**
☐ WHEEL LIFT   ☐ OUT OF GAS   ☐ SINGLE LINE WINCHING
☐ FLAT BED/RAMP   ☐ WRECK   ☐ DUAL LINE WINCHING
☐ START   ☐ RECOVERY   ☐ SNATCH BLOCKS
☐ LOCK OUT   ☐ ODOMETER READING   ☐ SCOTCH BLOCKS
☐ BLOCK DRIVEWAY ☐ ILLEGAL PARKING   ☐ DOLLY
                                       ☐ _____

LEFT SIDE   FRONT   BACK

RIGHT SIDE

I AUTHORIZE THE TOWING OF THE ABOVE VEHICLE

X _____

CAR WAS TOWED:	**DISTANCE TOWED:**	
FROM:	MILEAGE END	
TO:	MILEAGE START	
	TOTAL DISTANCE TOWED	
MEMBER # _____	MILEAGE CHARGE	
P.O.# _____	TOWING CHARGE	
REMARKS _____	LABOR CHARGE	
_____	STORAGE CHARGE	
_____	TOLLS	
VEHICLE RELEASED TO _____	TAX	
WITH NO FURTHER RECOURSE TO _____	**TOTAL**	

TOWING INVOICE

COMPANY NAME		24 HOUR TOWING SERVICE FLATBED SERVICE	
(STAMP)		REQ. BY:	
NAME		DATE	
ADDRESS		TIME	
CITY	STATE	ZIP	PHONE
YEAR	MAKE / MODEL / COLOR		DRIVER
STATE	LIC NO.	VEHICLE ID NO.	

- ☐ SLING/HOIST
- ☐ WHEEL LIFT
- ☐ FLAT BED/RAMP
- ☐ START
- ☐ LOCK OUT
- ☐ BLOCK DRIVEWAY

- ☐ FLAT TIRE
- ☐ OUT OF GAS
- ☐ WRECK
- ☐ RECOVERY
- ☐ ODOMETER READING
- ☐ ILLEGAL PARKING

SPECIAL EQUIPMENT
- ☐ SINGLE LINE WINCHING
- ☐ DUAL LINE WINCHING
- ☐ SNATCH BLOCKS
- ☐ SCOTCH BLOCKS
- ☐ DOLLY
- ☐ _____

LEFT SIDE   FRONT   BACK

RIGHT SIDE

I AUTHORIZE THE TOWING OF
THE ABOVE VEHICLE

X _____

CAR WAS TOWED:	DISTANCE TOWED:	
FROM:	MILEAGE END	
TO:	MILEAGE START	
	TOTAL DISTANCE TOWED	
MEMBER # _____	MILEAGE CHARGE	
P.O.# _____	TOWING CHARGE	
REMARKS _____	LABOR CHARGE	
_____	STORAGE CHARGE	
_____	TOLLS	
VEHICLE RELEASED TO _____	TAX	
WITH NO FURTHER RECOURSE TO _____	TOTAL	

NOTES

NOTES

Made in the USA
Las Vegas, NV
13 December 2024

14036271R10070